cave

DIANE SIEBERT • ILLUSTRATIONS BY WAYNE McLOUGHLIN

HarperCollins Publishers

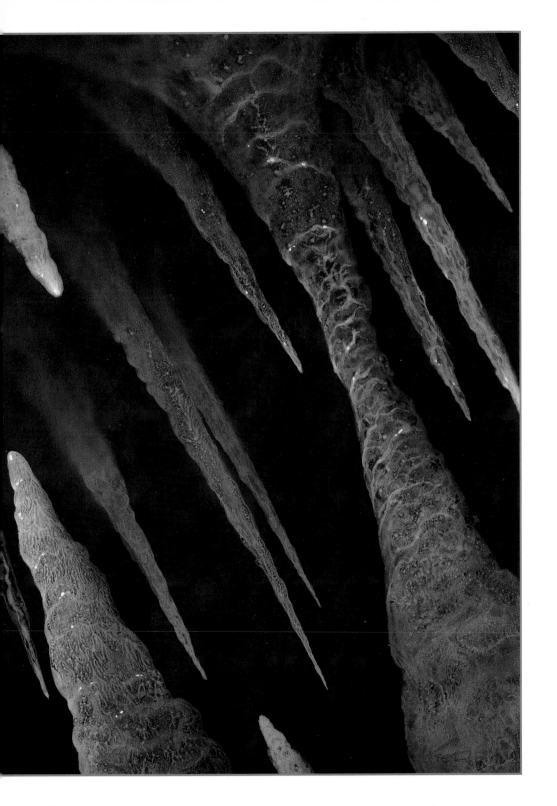

I am the cave,
So cool and dark,
Where time, unending, leaves its mark
As natural forces build and hone
A crystal world from weeping stone.

I am the cave,
And at my core
A sea once was that is no more—
A sea alive and sunlight-warmed
Where limestone, born of death, was
  formed
As sediment of shell and bone,
Compressed, became a floor of stone.
But shifting continents brought change;
This floor, upthrust, became a range
Of mountains that displaced the sea
And held the limestone heart of me.

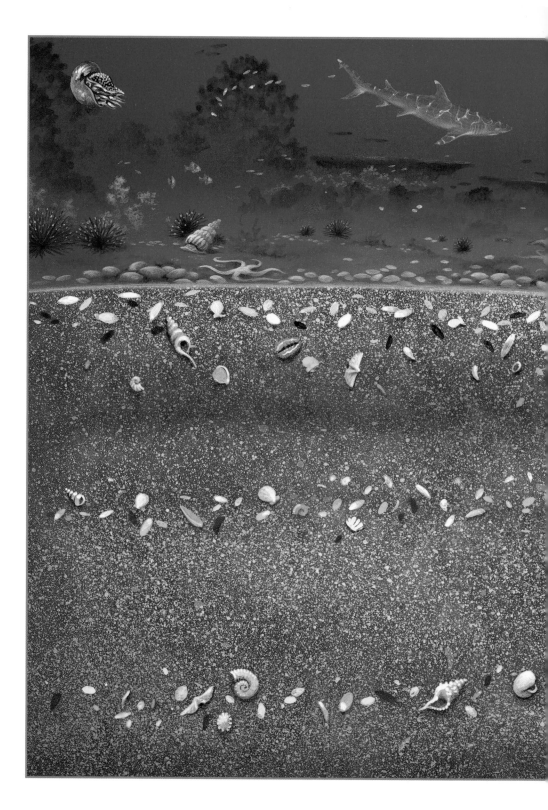

And through the eons I evolved,
My limestone, bit by bit, dissolved
By Nature's forces intertwined
In endless tears that left behind
The hollows that grew long and wide—
A cave within the mountainside.

I am the cave,
   Now changed and grown,
Where that which once dissolved the
   stone,
In slow reversal now creates
New stone that fills and decorates
This inner world—a hidden maze
Of chambers linked by passageways.

My ceilings cry their endless tears
That fall throughout the endless years,
Each droplet leaving just a trace
Of sparkling crystal in its place.

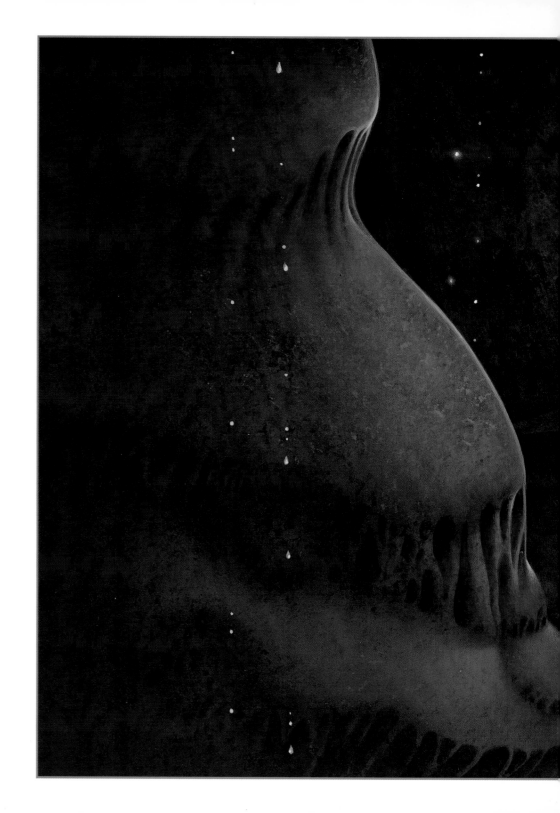

And here and there my ceilings hold
The draperies whose shapes unfold
As water follows fissured trails
And crystals form translucent veils.

And other charms of stone exist:
Helictites spiral, turn, and twist,
While hardened streams of flowstone
   spill
Like waterfalls, alive yet still;
And rimstone dams hold little pools
Amid my "pearl" and "coral" jewels.

I am the cave,
  Dark, damp, and chill,
Where forms of life evolved to fill
This niche, whose mazes, reaching back,
Progress from bright to blackest black.

My entrance welcomes many guests
And holds the little muddy nests
Of swallows that dart gracefully
Around that sunlit space of me.

Inside, where light fades into gloom,
A twilight place—an anteroom—
Greets trogloxenes who feed outside
But venture in to rest, to hide:
The snakes, the porcupines, the rats,
The skunks, the mice, and ah! the bats....

Each time I feel the day begin,
A rush of wings comes sweeping in,
And soon my ceilings teem with those
Who hang in upside-down repose
And who, in search of insects, fly
When darkness claims the evening sky.

But unlike guests who come and go,
Some creatures choose to stay below,
For darkness, cool and damp, beguiles
These cavern-loving troglophiles:
The crickets without wings and voice,
And salamanders who, by choice,
Remain within where they can shun
All hint of day, all trace of sun.

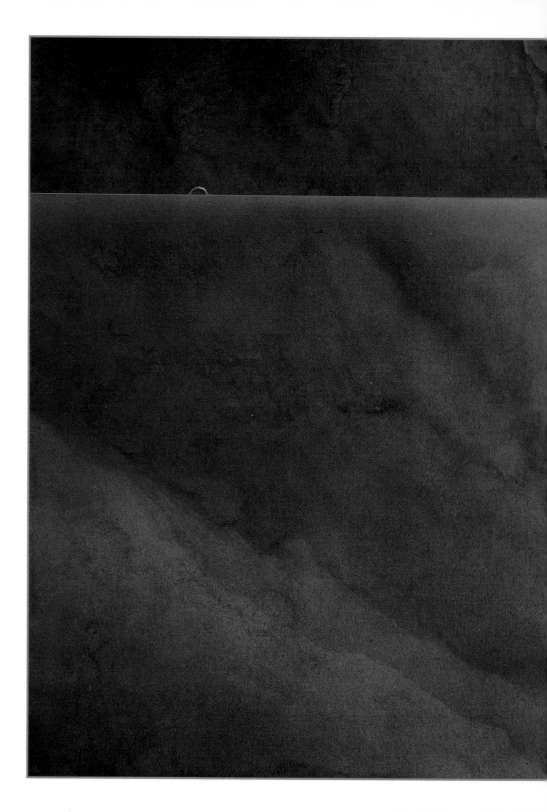

And in those depths untouched by light,
In places darker than the night,
All hues are lost, eyes cannot see,
And troglobites have come to be;
These creatures, pale and blind,
 have found
No need for sight beneath the ground,
And sightless, they can never leave,
But with their other gifts perceive
The unseen world in which they dwell—
A world of hearing, touch, and smell.

I know these little troglobites:
White beetles, millipedes, and mites;
White crayfish whose antennae guide
Them through my stream, where
 blindfish glide;
White spiders that so lightly crawl
From rock to rock, from wall to wall.

I am the cave.
     Long have I known
Dark silhouettes on lamp-lit stone;
For humans, too, have journeyed here,
From early Man with torch and spear
To Man today, whose questing mind
Has reached into my depths to find
The secrets of what lies within
This realm, pristine and crystalline.

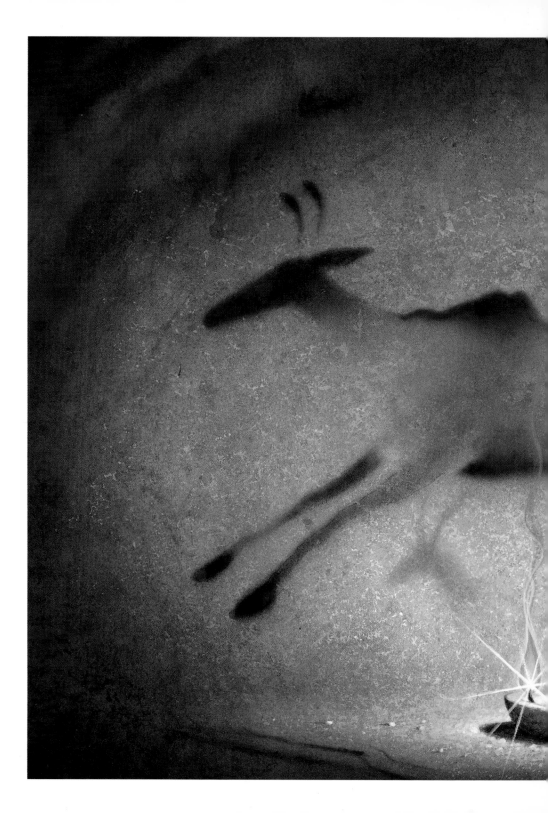

These humans, through technology,
Have shaped the land, the air, the sea;
Their skills have brought them great
   success,
Yet all the talents they possess
Cannot a crushed stalactite heal,
Effects of warmth and light conceal,
A shattered rimstone dam replace,
A trail of carelessness erase.
And knowing this, Man holds my fate
While I, beneath earth's surface, wait.

I am the cave,
So cool and dark,
Where time, unending, leaves its mark
As natural forces build and hone
A crystal world from weeping stone.

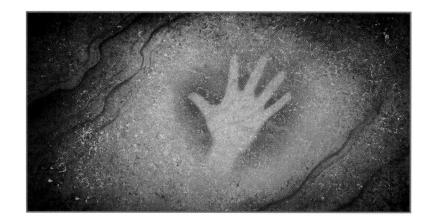

Author's Note

Limestone caves are wonders of nature—dark, mysterious, fragile, and incredibly beautiful. Many had their beginnings over five hundred million years ago, when seas covered much of what is now land. For millions and millions of years, small creatures that lived in those seas died and sank to the bottom, where their bones and shells piled up in layers hundreds of feet thick. Each layer was compressed by the weight of the layer on top and eventually turned to limestone rock. After millions of years more, as the earth's crust shifted, the rock began to rise and the seas drained away, leaving hills and mountains that today hold the limestone needed for Mother Nature's underground artistry.

There are thousands of caves found all over the world. Some are very small, just a few feet in diameter. Others are massive, composed of many rooms and extending for miles and miles beneath the earth's surface. There are developed caves with trails and electric lights that people can visit in safety with the help of guides, and there are undeveloped caves that, in their natural state, can be explored by expert cavers only. But best of all are the many undiscovered caves hidden underground, the ones safe from humankind's often destructive touch. For despite the passage of various laws to protect them, caves and the creatures they shelter continue to be damaged and destroyed at an alarming rate.

Perhaps some caves should forever remain beyond our reach and in our imaginations only.